From Trash to Treasures

Paper

Daniel Nunn

Heinemann Library
Chicago, Illinois

www.heinemannraintree.com
Visit our website to find out
more information about
Heinemann-Raintree books.

To order:
☎ Phone 888-454-2279
💻 Visit www.heinemannraintree.com
to browse our catalog and order online.

© 2011 Heinemann Library
an imprint of Capstone Global Library, LLC
Chicago, Illinois

Edited by Rebecca Rissman, Daniel Nunn, and
Sian Smith
Designed by Joanna Hinton-Malivoire
Picture research by Tracy Cummins
Originated by Capstone Global Library Ltd
Printed and bound in China by South China
Printing Company Ltd

15 14 13 12 11
10 9 8 7 6 5 4 3 2 1

**Library of Congress Cataloging-in-Publication
Data**
Nunn, Daniel.
  Paper / Daniel Nunn. —1.
     pages cm.—(From Trash to Treasures)
  Includes bibliographical references and index.
  ISBN 978-1-4329-5151-1 (hb)—ISBN 978-1-4329-
5160-3 (pb) 1. Paper work—Juvenile literature. 2.
Waste paper—Recycling—Juvenile literature. I. Title.
  TT870.N865 2011
  745.592—dc22   2010049826

Acknowledgments
We would like to thank the following for permission
to reproduce photographs: Alamy pp. 9, 23a
(Vincent L. Long), 22a (© Carole Hewer);
Heinemann Raintree pp. 4 (David Rigg), 5, 6, 10, 11,
12, 13, 14, 15, 16, 17, 18, 19, 20, 21, 23b, 23c (Karon
Dubke); Shutterstock pp. 7 (© Picsfive), 8, 23d (©
Patty Orly), 22b (© Nattika), 22c (© spaxiax).

Cover photograph of paper sack reproduced
with permission of istockphoto (© René Mansi).
Cover image of paper maché reproduced with
permission of Shutterstock (Andrew Olscher).
Back cover photographs of a coaster and a mask
reproduced with permission of Heinemann Raintree
(Karon Dubke).

Every effort has been made to contact copyright
holders of material reproduced in this book. Any
omissions will be rectified in subsequent printings if
notice is given to the publisher.

Disclaimer
All the Internet addresses (URLs) given in this book
were valid at the time of going to press. However,
due to the dynamic nature of the Internet, some
addresses may have changed, or sites may have
changed or ceased to exist since publication. While
the author and publisher regret any inconvenience
this may cause readers, no responsibility for any
such changes can be accepted by either the
author or the publisher.

Contents

Some words are shown in bold, **like this**. You can find them in the glossary on page 23.

What Is Paper?

Paper is a **material** we write on.

Paper is made from trees.

Books, magazines, newspapers, and notepads are all made of paper.

Napkins, plates, and cups can all be made of paper, too!

What Happens When You Throw Paper Away?

Paper is very useful.

But when you have finished with it, do you throw it away?

If you throw paper away, it will end up at a garbage dump.

It will be buried in the ground and may stay there for a very long time.

What Is Recycling?

It is much better to **recycle** paper instead of throwing it away.

Separate paper from your other trash and then put it in a recycling bin.

The paper will be collected and taken to a **factory**.

Then the paper will be made into something new.

How Can I Reuse Old Paper?

You can also use old paper to make your own new things.

When you have finished with something made out of paper, put it aside instead of throwing it away.

Soon you will have lots of paper waiting
to be reused.

You are ready to turn your trash
into treasures!

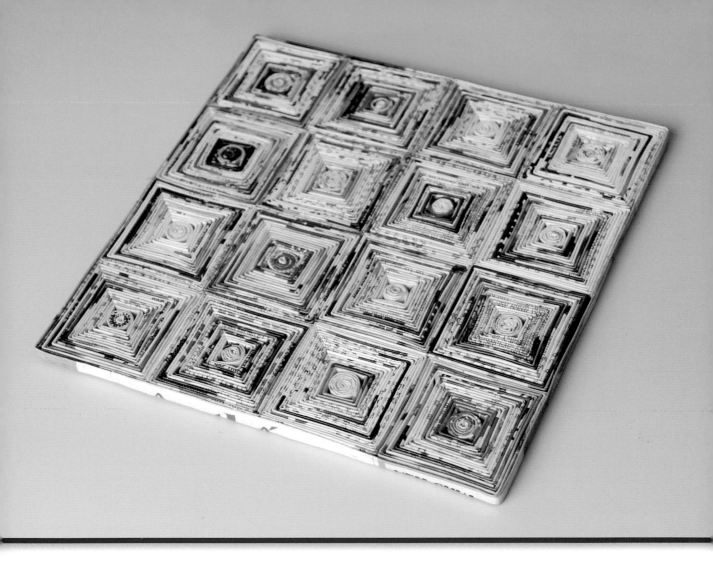

Magazines can be made into colorful coasters.

This coaster has been made by folding up pages from magazines.

You can also cut up paper to make beautiful **mosaics**.

This picture of a bird is made out of lots of tiny pieces of old paper.

What Can I Make with Paper Cups and Bags?

You can use an old paper cup to make a fun ball-and-cup game.

Try to catch the ball in the cup—it is harder than it looks!

Paper bags make great puppets!

What sort of paper bag puppet will you make?

What Else Can I Make with Paper?

You can make all sorts of things with **paper maché**.

These children are wearing paper maché masks.

Making paper maché can be a little messy.

Try to keep clean by wearing an apron made of old newspapers!

Make Your Own Magazine Nameplate

You can use old magazines to make a nameplate for your bedroom door.

You will need a piece of cardboard, scissors, glue, and old magazines.

First, decide what you want your nameplate to say.

Then, cut out the letters that you need from the magazines. Do not use sharp scissors without help from an adult.

Arrange the letters in the correct order on the cardboard.

Then, carefully glue each letter to the cardboard.

Wait for the glue to dry.

Your nameplate is ready to be put on your bedroom door!

Recycling Quiz

One of these things is made from **recycled** paper. Can you guess which one? (The answer is on page 24.)

Glossary

 **factory** building where something is made

 **material** what something is made of

 **mosaic** picture made from small pieces of paper, glass, or tiles

 **paper maché** mixture of shredded paper and glue used to make things. It gets hard when it is dry.

 **recycle** break down a material and use it again to make something new

Find Out More

Ask an adult to help you make fun things with paper using the Websites below.

Ball-and-cup game: **www.lakeshorelearning. com/general_content/free_resources/crafts/mt_ catchthebead.jsp**

Fruits and vegetables: **http://familyfun.go.com/crafts/ papier-mache-veggies-661990/**

Coasters**: www.clevernesting.com/2009/07/recycled- magazine-page-coaster-tutorial/**

Answer to question on page 22
The cat is made from recycled paper.

Index